1. An M4A1 (76mm) takes part in the fighting in the Ardennes on 11 January. Even the newer 76mm gun on the Sherman was by no means adequate to deal with heavier German tanks such as the Panther or Royal Tiger.

Battle of the Bulge

STEVEN J. ZALOGA

a&
ap

ARMS AND ARMOUR PRESS
London — Melbourne — Harrisburg. Pa

Introduction

Tanks Illustrated 2: Battle of the Bulge
Published in 1983 by
Arms and Armour Press, Lionel Leventhal Limited,
2-6 Hampstead High Street, London NW3 1QQ;
4-12 Tattersalls Lane, Melbourne, Victoria 3000,
Australia; Cameron and Kelker Streets,
P.O. Box 1831, Harrisburg, Pennsylvania 17105,
USA

British Library Cataloguing in Publication Data:
Zaloga, Steven J.
Battle of the Bulge. – (Tanks illustrated; 2)
1. World War, 1939–1945 – Campaigns – Ardennes
(France) – Pictorial works.
2. World War, 1939–1945 – Tank warfare – Pictorial
works.
I. Title   II. Series
940.54′ 21′ 0222   DA756.5.A7
ISBN 0-85368-581-9

Layout by Anthony A. Evans.
Printed in Great Britain by William Clowes,
Beccles, Limited.

The popular image of the Battle of the Bulge focuses on the heroic defence of Bastogne by the paratroopers of the 101st Airborne Division. Nevertheless, like most of the other battles in northwest Europe, the fighting in the Ardennes was dominated by armoured actions, whether the initial German armoured attacks of 16 December, the dramatic race to the Meuse by Kampfgruppe Peiper, the defence of St. Vith, Krinkelt and Rocherath by infantry backed by tanks and tank destroyers, or the impressive drive of the 4th Armored Division to relieve Bastogne. The aim of this book is to provide photographic coverage of the armoured equipment and armoured units that took part in the fighting in the Ardennes.

Not surprisingly, there are gaps. German coverage is very thin, due no doubt to the secrecy that surrounded the preparations for the Ardennes offensive. There are a handful of well known photographs of the German attack on 16 and 17 December that appear in nearly every book on the subject, and these have been omitted intentionally. The major sources of German military photographs, the US National Archives, the Bundesarchiv Koblenz and the French ECP Armée collection, are nearly devoid of photographs of the Ardennes fighting. As a result, the illustrations of German armoured equipment included here are nearly all from the American perspective, and depict vehicles knocked out during the course of the fighting.

While American coverage of the fighting is far more comprehensive, it is by no means complete. It will become apparent that coverage of the first two weeks of fighting in December 1944 is by no means as thorough as that in January. Once the US Army went over to the counter-offensive, the situation improved. This is not surprising in view of the confusion and chaos of the early skirmishes in December. As a result, the photographic coverage here lacks views of the 7th Armored Division's heroic resistance around St. Vith in December, but does cover the division during its counterattacks on St. Vith in January. Similarly, coverage of the 4th Armored Division's dash to relieve Bastogne around Christmas is very thin, while its later actions around Bastogne are better covered. When I asked Colonel James Leach, a veteran of 4th Armored, why this was the case, he replied simply that no photographers were allowed to accompany the task force in view of the dangerous nature of the assignment. In spite of these gaps, this book represents the most thorough photographic coverage yet published of armoured equipment employed during the Ardennes fighting. Unless otherwise noted, all photographs are from the US Signals Corps, located in the collections at the US Army Still Photographic Library or at the Still Photographic Library of the US National Archives.

Steven J. Zaloga, 1983

2. The crew of an M5A1 light tank of B Company, 759th Tank Battalion eat K-rations while warming themselves by a fire on 30 December 1944. The crew's Thompson submachine-guns are close to hand, resting against a tree.

△3 ▽4

5△

3. US troops advanced into Belgium in September 1944. These GIs of the 9th Infantry Division, photographed on 9 September 1944 are being supported by an M4 Sherman tank, which is still fitted with 'rhino' prongs used to push through the hedgerows of Normandy a month earlier.

4. German infantry cling to the back of a Jagdpanzer IV during the initial attacks on 16 December. Many areas were not snow covered during this early phase in the fighting, hence the speckled 'ambush pattern' camouflage sported by this tank destroyer, believed to have belonged to SS-Pz Jag Abt 1, fighting with Kampfgruppe Hansen on 17–18 December 1944.

5. A German Royal Tiger tank rolls through a Belgian village during the opening hours of the Ardennes offensive. The Royal Tiger proved to be a problem for American troops, since no US tank gun could penetrate its thick frontal armour. Only the 90mm gun of the M36 tank destroyer was effective, though Royal Tigers could be knocked out by flank shots. (J.-P. Pallud via B. Auerbach)

6. Another view of a Royal Tiger in operation in an Ardennes town during the first day of fighting. (J.-P. Pallud via Bill Auerbach)

6▽

△7

7. A battery of 15cm SIG 33/1 Grille self-propelled howitzers bombard American positions, 17 December 1944. This particular photograph was captured from the Germans by troops of the 3rd Armored Division later in the fighting.

8. A Royal Tiger tank believed to be of 1st SS Panzer Division during the initial German advances on 17 December 1944.

9. A pair of Panther Ausf G tanks knocked out in the streets of Krinkelt during the fighting there on 17 December 1944. In the narrow streets of Krinkelt and Rocherath, the 12th SS Panzer Division lost many tanks to roving bazooka teams as well as to hidden tank destroyers.

10, 11. A German Panther Ausf G tank burns after being hit in the side of the turret by a bazooka round from a 2nd Infantry Division team. This tank formed part of the 12th SS Panzer Division drive towards Krinkelt on 17 December.

△8 ▽9

12. SS troops advance in the Ardennes on the engine deck of an Sd Kfz 234/1 armoured car on 17 December 1944.
13. In an attempt to bluff their way through American positions, the Germans formed Panzer Brigade 150, a special unit commanded by the famous Otto Skorzeny, which was equipped with captured American uniforms and equipment or German equipment disguised as American vehicles. Its tanks were mainly Panthers elaborately disguised to resemble US M10 tank destroyers. This example was destroyed outside Malmédy.

△12 ▽13

14. Panzer Brigade 150 was not used extensively in its intended role, but instead was committed to the fight to dislodge American infantry dug-in in Malmédy on 21 December 1944. The attack was a shambles with most of the disguised Panther/M10s being destroyed by bazooka teams or artillery.

15. Another view of a disguised Panther of Panzer Brigade 150 disabled in the Malmédy fighting shows the thin sheet metal turret panels added to make the tank more closely resemble an American tank destroyer. On this tank, the turret has been reversed and the rear panel removed to permit the crew to escape.

16. Besides Panther tanks, Panzer Brigade 150 also used StuG IIIs. These bore little resemblance to any American vehicle, but were painted in olive drab with white stars in a vain attempt to confuse inexperienced American troops. This particular vehicle was knocked out near Geromont.

14△

15△ 16▽

△17

△18 ▽19

17. A Panther Ausf G tank of 1st SS Panzer Division knocked out in Malmédy not far from the scene of the infamous massacre in which over 70 captured Americans were shot by Peiper's SS troops.

18. An Sd Kfz 250 half-track in American markings – believed to have been one of the vehicles of Panzer Brigade 150 – abandoned in Regne by the Germans after having been booby-trapped.

19. GIs inspect a Pz Kpfw IV Ausf J knocked out by M10 tank destroyers during the US withdrawal from Wirtzfeld on 17 December 1944.

20. An M4A1 medium tank of the 3rd Armored Division concealed behind a road-block at Manhay on 23 December. Positions around this vital crossroads were held by elements of the 3rd and 7th Armored Divisions.

21. M36 90mm tank destroyers of the 703rd Tank Destroyer Battalion rushing to Werbomont to support the 82nd Airborne Division on 20 December. The 82nd Airborne was facing Kampfgruppe Peiper and was desperately in need of the M36, which was the only US armoured vehicle with a gun large enough to deal effectively with the Royal Tigers used by Peiper's units.

△22

22. A Panther tank of the 2nd SS Panzer Division knocked out during the fighting near Manhay on 23 December 1944.

23. The crew of a British Sherman Firefly guard the bridge at Namur on Christmas Day to prevent its capture by German paratroopers. Although German paratroop drops had little tactical success, they did tie up many troops such as these.

24. A British Sherman crew mans a crossroads in Namur and checks the papers of some American war correspondents in a Dodge 3/4-ton weapons carrier.

25. A Panther Ausf G and a Pz Kpfw IV of the 116th Panzer Division destroyed by American infantry during the fighting in Hotton, 26 December 1944.

26. A Pz Kpfw IV Ausf H named 'Lustmolch' which was knocked out by troops of the 101st Airborne when it tried to break into Bastogne on 26 December.

△23 ▽24

△27

△28 ▽29

27. The armoured troops in surrounded Bastogne had no access to paint with which to whitewash their vehicles, thus calling for some alternative camouflage measures. White bed linen provided the answer for this M3A1 half-track of the 10th Armored Division.

28. An M7B1 105mm HMC takes up a firing position along the highway to Manhay on 27 December. This SP howitzer belonged to the 7th Armored Division, which finally succeeded in halting the advance of the 2nd SS Panzer Division on 26–27 December by the recapture of Manhay. By this time, the 7th Armored was down to 40 per cent of its strength.

29. An M4A3 (76mm) of the 19th Tank Battalion, 9th Armored Division advances to Bastogne during the drive to widen the corridor into the besieged town on 27 December 1944.

30. The crew of an M4 105mm assault gun scan the road near Manhay for further counterattacks by the 2nd SS Panzer Division. The dogged resistance of the 7th Armored since its initial efforts at St. Vith were a major factor in the US Army's success in holding the northern shoulder of the bulge. The 105mm assault gun was a version of the M4 Sherman tank used in tank battalions to provide fire support in place of the open-topped M7 105mm HMC.

31. An M36 tank destroyer hidden in a ditch covers a road overlooking Manhay on 27 December 1944. During the Ardennes fighting, the M36 proved to be a much cherished piece of equipment since it was the only armoured vehicle capable of dealing with the heavier German tank types.

34△

35△ 36▽

32. These three Panther Ausf G tanks of the 9th Panzer Division were among the victims of the 2nd Armored Division's attack on Humain on 26–27 December 1944.

33. An M4A1 (76mm) medium tank of the 2nd Armored Division loaded with troops of 2/291 Infantry preparing to push off for Frandeux during the battle for Humain, 27 December. It is worth mentioning that much of Belgium was not yet snow-covered, contrary to the popular conception of the Ardennes fighting. During the fight against the 47th Panzer Corps around Humain, the 2nd Armored Division accounted for 82 panzers, 83 assault guns and 441 other vehicles for a loss of 5 M5A1 light tanks and 22 M4 mediums.

34. A German Pz Kpfw IV tank rests in the ruins of Don Butenbach, having been knocked out in an attack on the positions of the 1st Infantry Division. To the left can be seen the front of a camouflaged American M36 tank destroyer.

35. An M4 105mm assault gun tank towing an M10 ammunition trailer passes through Habay-la-Neuve during the 6th Armored Division's drive to relieve Bastogne, 29 December 1944.

36. An M3 half-track of the 6th Armored Division on 29 December 1944 in Habay-la-Neuve. The 6th Armored Division was one of the three armoured divisions committed to widening the corridor into Bastogne from the southern edge of the bulge, the others being the 4th Armored and parts of the 9th Armored Division.

▲37

▲38 ▽39

37. An M15A1 MGMC of Battery D, 197th AAA Battalion guards a bridge from air attack in Limbourg. The battle for the Ardennes was one of the last occasions when Luftwaffe ground attack aircraft posed a serious threat to Allied ground formations, and M15 and M16 multiple-gun motor carriages played an important role in repulsing these attacks.

38. Half-tracks of the 10th Armored Division are camouflaged with bed sheets obtained while the unit was still trapped in Bastogne.

39. A victim of the relief drive on Bastogne, this M18 tank destroyer lies burned-out by the roadside. In the background is an M15A1 MGMC keeping an eye open for marauding German aircraft, 29 December.

40. A disabled Panther Ausf G of the 2nd SS Panzer Division after the town of Grandmenil was taken by the 3rd Armored Division in late December.

41. M4 105mm assault gun tanks of the HQ Company, 750th Tank Battalion provide support from camouflaged positions outside Manhay on 30 December during the battle to hold the region from attacks by the 2nd SS Panzer Division.

△ 42

42. An M36 90mm tank destroyer lurks behind a ruined building in Hotton on 30 December. The 116th Panzer Division had been pushed out of Hotton on Christmas Day, and was later held by infantry backed up by the 628th Tank Destroyer Battalion.

43. A Pz Kpfw VI Royal Tiger of Kampfgruppe Peiper knocked out in the streets of Stavelot during the fighting there serves as a reminder of the 1st SS Panzer Division.

44. An M25 Dragon Wagon retrieves an M4 medium tank of the 4th Armored Division knocked out during the drive to relieve Bastogne. The Sherman was destroyed by two direct hits in the hull side. This photograph demonstrates why many American tanks had their conspicuous American star insignia removed – it made a good aiming point for German anti-tank guns!

43 △   44 ▽

△45 ▽46

45. The crew of an M4 105mm assault gun tank of the 5th Armored Regiment open up their Christmas packages near Eupen on 30 December 1944.
46. M4 medium tanks of the 35th Tank Battalion, 4th Armored Division deploy in a clearing near Sainlex on 31 December 1944 during the fighting around Bastogne.

47. The crew of an M15A1 MGMC and troops of the 101st Airborne warm themselves by a fire on 31 December 1944. The M15A1 belonged to the 777th AAA Battalion, which provided air defence in Bastogne.
48. An M7B1 105mm HMC of the 274th AFAB prepares to fire in support of troops outside Bastogne, 1 January 1945.

47△ 48▽

△49

49. The crew of an M16 MGMC await instructions while supporting attacks of the 11th Armored Division near Neufchâteau, 1 January 1945. This half-track is still in its summer camouflage of black swathes over olive drab. On the forward winch are a number of liberated jerrycans.

50. An M4A3 passes by a disabled Panther of the 2nd SS Panzer Division outside Grandmenil, 2 January 1945.

51. British infantry advance in Bren Carriers near Marche, Belgium, 2 January 1945. The vehicle in the foreground is armed with a PIAT.

52. M4 105mm assault gun tanks of the 2nd Battalion, 32nd Armored Regiment, 3rd Armored Division fire on German positions near Trou-de-Bra on 3 January 1945. The area behind them is littered with the fibreboard packing containers in which the ammunition was stowed.

53. With heavy snowfalls in January, problems with armoured vehicles skidding on roads increased. Chains are being used here to give this half-track greater traction.

△50 ▽51

△54

△55 ▽56

54. A skirmish line of M4 medium tanks of the 35th Tank Battalion, 4th Armored Division take up defensive positions after being backed up by M10 tank destroyers along the Bastogne corridor near highway N-4, 3 January 1945.

55. A .30 calibre Browning light machine-gun team is passed by an M4 medium tank of the 4th Armored Division in the Bastogne Corridor, 3 January 1945.

56. A brand new M4A3E8 of the 4th Armored Division guards the N-4 highway outside Bastogne on 8 January 1945. This new version of the Sherman had a new suspension and wider tracks which offered better performance in deep snow. The white star on the turret has been over-painted.

57. A Panther Ausf G of the 2nd SS Panzer Division is inspected by tankers of the 2nd Armored Division in the woods near Grandmenil where it was disabled in the fighting late in December.

57▽

△58 ▽59

58. An M4A1 81mm mortar carrier provides fire support for the advance of the 2nd Armored Division on the outskirts of Amonines, 4 January 1945. The M4 was designed with the 81mm mortar firing over the rear, but the 2nd Armored Division modified its M4s and M4A1s to fire forward.

59. A 3/4-ton Dodge ambulance passes one of the disabled Royal Tigers of Kampfgruppe Peiper, 4 January 1945.

60. An M4 medium tank crew replenishes its ammunition supply with 75mm rounds near Jodenville, 5 January 1945.

61. A GI tries out a pair of captured German skis while an M10 tank destroyer in the background from 3rd Armored Division covers a road junction. A major short-coming of American tank destroyers was their unarmoured roof. In this case, the crew has added an improvised cover of logs over the turret opening to offer some protection from small arms fire and grenades.

60△ 61▽

△62

△63 ▽64

62. An artilleryman of Battery C, 274th AFAB fuzes a 105mm artillery round for the M7B1 in the background during the fighting around Bastogne, 5 January 1945.

63. A German Sd Kfz 251/3 command vehicle on fire near American lines in the Jodenville area, 6 January 1945. This was the command version of the Hanomag half-track, as is very evident from the prominent radio aerials at the rear.

64. A well camouflaged M7B1 105mm HMC of the 212th AFAB, 6th Armored Division provides fire support for its parent division on 8 January 1945. This particular battalion had established a record of 1,000 rounds per day, which was double the usual rate of fire.

65. M4s of the 3rd Armored Division advance with caution down a wooded road on 7 January 1945 during the counterattacks to seal the German bulge.

66. A column of Bren Carriers of the British 51st Highland Division advance cross-country around Leignon, 8 January 1945.

67. An M4A3 medium tank is recovered by an M25 Dragon Wagon and trailer in the wake of the fighting around Bastogne, 6 January 1945. This vehicle has received two direct hits on the turret.

65△

66△ 67▽

△68 ▽69

70△ 71▽

68. A Royal Tiger knocked out by tank destroyers of the 628th Tank Destroyer Battalion which was supporting the advance of the 82nd Airborne during the fighting around Coronne, 8 January 1945.

69. An armoured infantry unit of the 11th Armored Division prepares for action on the outskirts of Bastogne. The battle for the Ardennes was the baptism of fire for the new 11th Armored Division.

70. An M7B1 105mm HMC prepares for action during the fighting around Morhet on 9 January 1945. In the right foreground is an enormous pile of ammunition in its black fibreboard packing containers.

71. A column of the 750th Tank Battalion, 75th Infantry Division move up to relieve the 82nd Airborne near Basse Bodeaux on 10 January 1945. The leading M4 has steel cleat tracks and grousers for better snow traction.

72. 'Blockbuster III', the command tank of Captain James Leach of 'B' Company, 37th Tank Battalion, which took part in the lunge by the 37th Tank Battalion, 4th Armored Division to relieve Bastogne. 'Blockbuster' is seen here in January after being white-washed. (Col. J. Leach)

72▽

△73 ▽74

73. An M4 of the 750th Tank Battalion leads a column of infantry from the 75th Division as they move up to relieve the 82nd Airborne on 10 January 1945.

74. A GI inspects a Royal Tiger tank knocked out by flank fire from tanks of the 6th Armored Division during fighting near Wardin around 12 January 1945.

75△ 76▽

75. The crew of an M4A3 (76mm) keep their fingers crossed since this is their third tank in less than two weeks. The crew is commanded by Capt. John Megglesin (sitting on tank, right) and belonged to the 42nd Tank Battalion, 11th Armored Division.

76. Two armoured vehicles lie derelict after fighting in Wardin on 17 January 1945. The German Sd Kfz 251 half-track in ambulance markings was abandoned by its crew which took shelter in the adjacent church. The Sherman attacked the church at close range, but was disabled when a Panzerfaust blew off its left track. Eventually, other troops of the 6th Armored Division routed the Germans from the church.

77. A column of tanks of the 743rd Tank Battalion advance to the front through Malmédy on 13 January 1945. The leading vehicle is fitted with a dozer blade for clearing obstructions, and is heavily sandbagged as a form of improvised protection against German Panzerfaust anti-tank rockets. Behind it is one of the relatively rare M4A3E2 Jumbo assault tanks.

78. An M4A3 Sherman attached to the 492nd AFAB leaves Bastogne en route to Longchamps on 13 January. The vehicle is already bedecked in the de rigeur winter whitewash finish.
79. An M36 tank destroyer passes by a Pz Kpfw IV knocked out by the 3rd Armored Division during the fighting near Langlir on 13 January.

80. An M32 armoured recovery vehicle passes through the ruins of Bastogne while on its way to the front to support the 6th Armored Division. The M32 was a version of the M4A1 tank with recovery equipment for handling damaged tanks.

81. An M5A1 light tank of the 4th Cavalry Squadron passes by a knocked out Panther Ausf G medium tank on 9 January 1945.

82. M5A1 light tanks of the 37th Tank Battalion return from a patrol to the staging area of the 4th Armored Division in Bastogne on 14 January 1945. In the field can be seen some of the division's M18 tank destroyers.

△80

△81 ▽82

83△

83. A whitewashed half-track of the 11th Armored Division passes a Pz Kpfw IV disabled by a direct hit on its glacis plate at Foy on the outskirts of Bastogne.

84. An M4 medium tank knocked out during the attacks by the 10th Armored Division near Mageret on 15 January 1945. This was probably one of the 40 M4s of the 9th and 10th Armored Divisions that had been trapped inside Bastogne with the 101st Airborne during the siege.

85. The charred wreck of an M4A1 of the 69th Tank Battalion, 6th Armored Division knocked out by artillery near Wardin.

84△ 85▽

△86

86. This M4 of the 6th Armored Division was knocked out and suffered an internal explosion during the action against the 12th SS Panzer Division in the streets of Mageret on 4 January when control of the town changed hands after intense fighting.

87. An M29C Doodlebug in an unusually thorough splotch camouflage transports wounded soldiers of the 1st Infantry Division near Weywertz on 15 January 1945. These small tracked vehicles were specially designed for use on snow, but they were also amphibious and were used in small numbers in the Pacific theatre.

88. A tank platoon of the 11th Armored Division move forward in a field near Compogne on 15 January 1945. By this stage of the war, a large percentage of the Shermans in armoured divisions were of the newer, long barrelled 76mm version. Sometimes as much as 50 per cent of a unit might have the new improved versions, though in this case four of the six are so armed.

89. An M4A3 (76mm) passes a disabled German Pz Kpfw IV on the Houffalize road near Bertogne, 15 January 1945. The drive on Houffalize from north and south was intended to cut off the German bulge and trap as many German troops as possible.

90. GIs advance past a disabled German Flakpanzer IV Wirbelwind anti-aircraft tank during the fighting near Compogne on 15 January.

△87 ▽88

 △91 ▽92

91. One M32 ARV assists another in mounting on its front end a set of T1E1 mine rollers on 16 January 1945 during attempts to clear German anti-tank mines along the Faymonville road.
92. An M32 ARV equipped with a T1E1 mine roller proceeds down a road near Faymonville, 16 January 1945. These mine rollers were very cumbersome and not altogether popular with their users.
93. This M4 medium tank is having T1E3 'Aunt Jemima' mine

rollers attached for its initial combat trials near Wiesme, Belgium on 16 January 1945. The T1E3 used larger roller discs, hence the nickname derived from the popular American pancake mix.
94. A platoon of M4 105mm assault gun tanks with M10 ammunition trailers of the HQ Company, 774th Tank Battalion, 3rd Armored Division blend in the snow with their whitewash finishes, 16 January 1945.

△95

△96 ▽97

95. A mixed formation of the 702nd Tank Battalion, and 66th Armored Regiment, 2nd Armored Division await orders for an attack on Houffalize, 16 January 1945. In the foreground is an M36 90mm tank destroyer, behind it a 75mm gun M4A1 and, lastly, a 76mm armed M4A3 (76mm).

96. An M32 ARV fitted with a T1E1 mine roller assembly leads a column from the 2nd Armored Division while moving towards Houffalize, 16 January.

97. M4 medium tanks and an M5A1 light tank advance on a ridge during the 42nd Tank Battalion's drive on Mabompre on 16 January 1945.

98. A grimy M4A3 (76mm) of the 750th Tank Battalion passes through Salmchâteau while supporting the 75th Infantry Division on 16 January 1945. On the heap of personal stores and bedding at the rear is a fluorescent orange air identification panel, the standard means of Allied tank units to identify themselves to roving Allied fighter bombers.

99. The northern and southern pincers of the American drive that sealed the bulge arrived at a prearranged rendezvous on the Ourthe River near Houffalize on 16 January 1945, a month after the initial German attacks. Here, GIs of 84th Infantry Division shake hands with the crew of an M8 scout car of the 11th Armored Division's 41st Cavalry Squadron at about 08.45 on that historic day. Later in the morning, another 41st Cavalry Squadron patrol met elements of the 2nd Armored Division.

100. An M4A3 (76mm) passes by a knocked out Panther I near Bovigny on 17 January 1945 as American forces began to reduce German forces in the Ardennes.

101. Troops of the 30th Infantry Division near Pont await armour support as an M4A3E2 assault tank passes by. Even though more heavily armoured than normal Shermans, this assault tank is also heavily sand-bagged.

102. The crew of an M4A3 (76mm) whitewash their tank in Joubieval on 17 January 1945. This vehicle belonged to Company A, 774th Tank Battalion, which was supporting the 83rd Infantry Division at the time.

103. An M4 medium tank fitted with a T1E3 'Aunt Jemima' mine roller awaits orders to clear the road into Recht on 18 January 1945.

△99

△100 ▽101

102△ 103▽

△104

△105 ▽106

104. Paratroopers of the 82nd Airborne test bazookas on a pair of Royal Tigers of Kampfgruppe Peiper knocked out in La Gleize during the December fighting. These trials on 18 January 1945 only confirmed what most GIs already knew, that the bazooka was completely ineffective in penetrating the frontal armour of the Royal Tiger.

105. Wrecked German tanks litter the roadside near Bullingen after the fighting there in January. To the left is a Pz Kpfw IV and a Jagdpanther, and to the right can be seen a Jagdpanzer IV.

106. German troops made use of any mechanized equipment they could capture, such as this M8 armoured car that was finally knocked out by infantrymen of the 'Big Red One' (1st Infantry Division) in Faymonville, 18 January 1945.

107. One of the new tanks to enter service during the Ardennes fighting was the M24 Chaffee light tank, which replaced the earlier M5A1 in some units. This M24 of the 740th Tank Battalion, supporting the 82nd Airborne, was sent around to neighbouring US units to familiarize them with its appearance, which was very different from earlier American tank types due to its more modern torsion bar suspension.

108. An M10 tank destroyer of the 629th Tank Destroyer Battalion supporting the 83rd Infantry Division passes through Bovigny on 20 January 1945.

109. An M15A1 MGMC of the 778th AAA Battalion covers positions of the 3rd Armored Division outside Bastogne on 19 January 1945. These anti-aircraft units were made up of mixed companies of M16s and M15A1s, but with Luftwaffe targets dwindling in the last months of the war, they were used frequently to provide fire support to ground troops.

107△

108△ 109▽

△110

△111 ▽112

110. An M4 medium tank crew refuel their vehicle near Weims during the drive on St. Vith, 20 January 1945.

111. Whitewashed tanks of the 7th Armored Division move along the Edenbach road during the drive toward St. Vith. The 7th Armored Division had fought at St. Vith in the early stages of the Battle of the Bulge, and this attack took place on 20 January 1945.

112. Whitewashed half-tracks of the 44th Armored Infantry Battalion, 6th Armored Division rendezvous in a field near Mageret on 20 January 1945.

113△

113. The crew of an M10 tank destroyer of the 629th Tank Destroyer Battalion take a break in a wood near Courtil on 20 January 1945.

114. A Panther Ausf G knocked out by a tank destroyer from the 3rd Armored Division; Sterpigny, 20 January 1945. The Panther had been engaging a Sherman tank, which it hit, but in the meantime a tank destroyer crept up and disabled it from behind.

114▽

△115

△116 ▽117

115. A column of camouflaged M4A3s (76mm) advance to the front through Fisenne on 21 January 1945.

116. Troops of the 16th Infantry Regiment ride a tank during their advance on Schopen on 21 January. The usual practice when carrying infantry units was to mount half a squad per tank.

117. An M10 tank destroyer of the 773rd Tank Destroyer Battalion outside Benonchamps on 21 January. During earlier fighting near Oberwampach in Luxembourg, the 773rd had knocked out 103 German tanks, 5 of which were credited to this tank destroyer.

118. A column of armoured infantry move up towards the fighting in the Born area, 21 January 1945. Note that by this time, many GIs were wearing improvised snow camouflage.

119. Troops of the 504th Regiment (Airborne) supported by an M4A3 medium tank push through the snow near Herresbach.

△120

△121 ▽122

120. The crew of an M4 of the 6th Armored Division repair a track on their tank. During the Ardennes fighting, most American tanks were fitted with 'duck bill' grousers at the outer edge of the track to give better flotation in snow. However, these could be easily broken off and had to be repaired on occasion.

121. An M29 Doodlebug patrols a snow covered road near Schopen on 21 January. Also called the Weasel, this small utility vehicle was very useful in the later stages of the Ardennes fighting due to its exceptional flotation ability in deep snow which permitted it to travel in areas impassable to other vehicles.

122. An M18 tank destroyer of the 2nd Armored Division scoots around a bend near Fisenne on 21 January. The M18 was the lightest and fastest of American tank destroyers, but its 76mm gun was not as effective as the 90mm gun on the M36 tank destroyer.

123. Troops of the 16th Infantry Regiment use a captured German Sd Kfz 251/7 engineer half-track to transport supplies to the front lines near Schopen on 22 January. US infantry units were usually quite happy to use captured German half-tracks and other support vehicles, though their employment in the US Army was usually shortlived owing to a lack of suitable spares.

124. A German Opel Maultier half-track with a 105mm howitzer in tow abandoned near Wardin on the outskirts of Bastogne.

123△   124▽

△125

△126　▽127

125. A B-26 bomber crew hops into an M29 cargo carrier during their tour of the front lines to get a better understanding of the tactical air support requirements of the ground troops. In the background is an M10 tank destroyer.

126. An M4 Sherman with concrete armour on its glacis plate advances with infantry of the 75th Infantry Division during the attack on St. Vith from the Houffalize area. The tank belonged to the 750th Tank Battalion, which was supporting the 75th Infantry Division at the time.

127. Infantry and tanks of the 7th Armored Division are deployed in a field near Hunnange where they await orders for the final push against St. Vith. In the background are M4A1 and M4A3 mediums while in the foreground are M5A1 light tanks. By this point in the war the M5A1 was hopelessly undergunned and so usually was not brought to the fore where it was likely to encounter enemy armour.

128. A tanker of the 42nd Tank Battalion, 11th Armored Division sews his uniform while sitting in front of his M4 in the village of Steinbach, 23 January 1945. It is interesting to note that the left side track is nearly devoid of grousers while the right side appears to have a set intact.

129. Troops of the 23rd Infantry huddle behind an M4A3 Sherman as they advance through Hunnange on their way to St. Vith with the 7th Armored Division.

128△ 129▽

△130 ▽131

130. Although many heavy calibre artillery shells could not penetrate the armour of tanks, their high explosive force could certainly immobilize them. Here, a German StuG IV assault gun has been overturned by a near direct hit from American artillery near Amel on 24 January 1945.

131. A German Hetzer tank destroyer lies smouldering in the wreckage of the village of Wallerode near St. Vith having been hit moments before by tanks of the 7th Armored Division. The Hetzer was a sleek, small tank destroyer but was very thinly armoured as is evident in this view.

132. M4s of the 40th Tank Battalion, 7th Armored Division fire on German positions in the St. Vith area during the assault on the town, 24 January 1945.

133. Troops of the 509th Parachute Infantry Battalion, supported by an M5A1 light tank of the 7th Armored Division, push on against German positions beyond St. Vith, 24 January 1945.

△134 ▽135

134. An M4A3 Sherman of the 6th Armored Division named 'Ballero' lies abandoned after having been knocked out of action by a German anti-tank gun. The penetration of the tank can be seen aft the cartoon.

135. A German Flakpanzer IV lies abandoned by the roadside after the fighting in the Ardennes. This was a variant of the Pz Kpfw IV medium tank fitted with a new open-topped turret equipped with four 20mm automatic cannon for defence of mechanized columns against roving Allied fighter bombers.

136. A derelict Bergepanther sits by the roadside near Morhet on 27 January 1945. The Bergepanther was a recovery and repair version of the Panther tank. This particular vehicle is believed to be the one later shipped back to Aberdeen Proving Grounds in the US for inspection.

137. An M8 scout car captured by the Germans during the fighting near St. Vith in December 1944 and impressed into Wehrmacht service was later recaptured after having been hit by American artillery during the counter-offensive in February 1945.

138. The M29 frequently was used as an ambulance during the Battle of the Bulge, since it could travel in areas inaccessible to jeeps. Here, a Weasel recovers wounded of the 1st Infantry Division near Hepscheid on 28 January.

136△

137△ 138▽

△139

139. A combined tank/paratrooper column advances down a wooded road near Herresbach on 28 January. The paratroopers were from the 504th Regiment of the 82nd Airborne Division.

140. An M4 Sherman tank uses its dozer blade to clear a stretch of the road to Muringen. This tank belonged to the 745th Tank Battalion. Heavy snows late in January slowed the pace of the American counter-offensive in the Ardennes.

141. Bastogne remained a hub of activity during the American counter-offensive in the Ardennes in late January 1945. Here, an armoured field artillery battalion of M7B1 105mm HMC moves up to the front flanked by two 1/2-ton trucks.

△140 ▽141